PRISONERS OF WAR IN DARTMOOR TOWNS
French and American Officers on Parole 1803–1815

For Claire, Rosie and Alice.
With love from Grandad.

'Read and Learn'.

Photographs from author's collection unless otherwise acknowledged.

First published in Great Britain in 2000

Copyright © Trevor James 2000

ISBN 1 898964 39 4

ORCHARD PUBLICATIONS
2   Orchard Close, Chudleigh, Newton Abbot, Devon TQ13 0LR
Telephone: (01626) 852714

Printed by:
Hedgerow Print, Lapford, Crediton, Devon EX17 6AE

ACKNOWLEDGEMENTS

The author wishes to thank the following persons and organisations whose help was so freely given in the preparation of this book.

Ashburton Museum.
Bodmin Army Museum.
Grand Lodge of England, London.
Launceston Library.
Lawrence House Museum, Launceston.
Leicester Lodge of Research, Freemasons Hall, Leicester.
Moretonhampstead Parochial Church Council.
Okehampton Library.
Plymouth City Library – Local Studies.
Public Records Office, Coxside, Plymouth.
Tavistock Library.
Westcountry Studies Library, Exeter.
The Editor, *Western Morning News*, Plymouth.
Mr. N. Overton, Maritime History Officer, Plymouth City Museum.
Prison Officer Mike Chamberlain, H.M.P. Dartmoor.
The late Mr. Ron Chudley, Exmouth.
Mr. and Mrs. George Cole, formerly of Princetown.
Mr. Ira Dye (Author), Mill Valley, California, U.S.A.
Mr. Robin Fenner, Tavistock.
Mr. and Mrs. R. Freeman, North Tawton.
Mr. George Friend, Chagford.
Mr. and Mrs. A. Hope, Ashburton.
The late Mr. H.R. Horne, Okehampton.
The Rev. W. Leigh and Mrs. Leigh, Moretonhampstead.
Mrs. Wendy Major, Ashburton.
Monsieur R. Martin, Versailles, France.
The late Dr. R. Taverner, Exeter.
Col. F. Theobold, Moretonhampstead.
Mrs. E. Thomson (Researcher), Public Records Office, Kew.

CONTENTS

FOREWORD

The 'Parole' system evolved during the 18th. and early 19th. century wars with France and the United States, from the Seven Years War and the American War of Independence, remaining in force up until the Napoleonic Wars and the War of 1812 (often referred to by Americans as the 'Second War of Independence'). Under the terms of the parole agreement army and navy prisoners of war of certain ranks were encouraged to live amongst the people as ordinary citizens, subject to certain conditions.

In Britain a number of places were designated 'Parole Towns' where accommodation was made available for them. As the wars dragged on the population of towns and villages all over the country swelled as these foreign people with their foreign ways came to live among the inhabitants. Information concerning this period in our history is sparse and the researcher has to look into every nook and cranny of our libraries to find the briefest reference to isolated incidents, not always related to the locality under investigation. The prisoner of war lists at the Public Record Offices are a prime source of detail concerning certain prisoners who attained some notoriety or to obtain statistics about the number of escapes. Then there are the parish records where the occasional references to deaths, burials, marriages, etc. concerning the Frenchmen and others are mentioned. The best and most informative account of all aspects of the French prisoner's confinement in this country is Francis Abell's *French Prisoners of War in Britain 1756 - 1815* and it has been a close perusal of this volume which has yielded much of the inforrnation related here as well as clues for further enquiries. Francis Abell must have spent a lot of money and time travelling all over Britain in his quest for material, and his enthusiasm for his work manifests itself on every page; it is an essential book of reference for those interested in this aspect of our history. The stories he relates may not stand up to the strict guidelines of a professional historian, but they are taken from written and verbal recollections handed down in families and in the localities where they occurred, by those who actually witnessed what took place.

In general the prisoner's stay was a genial one and several life long friendships resulted. Inevitably there were love affairs, marriages, and children born. Some prisoners died and were buried in our churchyards, leaving their names in the parish records for all to see; yet very few people, even those living in the former parole towns today, are aware that such events ever took place and express a keen interest when it is made known to them. This little book is intended to fill a gap in our local history and hopefully arouse further interest in a colourful and fascinating era.

INTRODUCTION.

On the right hand side of the Tavistock to Whitchurch road, just above Crelake Park, there is a very old oak tree, the last in a line of trees. It is known as the 'Honour Oak' and the plaque fixed to its ivy-covered trunk testifies that this was the limit to which the French officers who were prisoners of war on Parole in Tavistock were permitted to go. The inscription reads:

HONOUR OAK TREE

Marked the boundary of French prisoners on parole in Tavistock from Princetown during the Napoleonic War 1803–1814.

The Honour Oak Plaque, Tavistock

The General Entry List for prisoners of war on parole in Tavistock for this period is missing from the files at the Public Record Office in Kew, but although accounts from other sources differ, it seems there were on average 150 officers on parole in Tavistock at any one time during the war. To help alleviate the overcrowding in the Prisoner of War Depots, and in deference to their rank, certain officers and other 'prisoners of quality' were permitted to live in selected towns as free citizens providing they gave their word of honour not to try to escape. During the Napoleonic Wars there were over 80 such towns in Britain – the actual number varied depending on the number of prisoners to be catered for. In the Dartmoor area the main Parole towns were Tavistock, Ashburton, Okehampton, North Tawton, Moretonhampstead, and Launceston. American officers were quartered at Reading and Ashburton with a small number at Dartmouth.

Parole Towns in 1803

Abergavenny	Hawick	Odiham
Alresford	Jedurgh	Okehampton
Andover	Kelso	Oswestry
Ashbourne	Lanark	Peebles
Ashburton	Lauder	Peterborough
Ashby-de-la-Zouch	Launceston	Reading
Biggar	Leek	Sanquhar
Bishop's Castle	Lichfield	Selkirk
Bishop's Waltham	Llanfyllin	South Molton
Brecon	Loch Maben	Tavistock
Bridgnorth	Lockerbie	Thame
Chesterfield	Melrose	Tiverton
Chippenham	Montgomery	Wantage
Crediton	Moreton Hampstead	Welshpool
Cupar	Newtown	Whitchurch (Salop)
Dumfries	Northampton	Wincanton
Hambledon	North Tawton	

From *Prisoners of War in Britain 1756–1815* (Francis Abell) by kind permission of Oxford University Press.

The inhabitants of these places, most of whom had never ventured further than the next town or village in their lives, were astonished at the strange sights they saw when their streets were 'invaded' by foreign officer prisoners of war, many of them attired in a colourful array of exotic uniforms. In some places there were captives from the nations who were allied to France at various times during the conflicts – dark eyed Spaniards whose appearance contrasted sharply with the pale faced Danes with their fair hair, and the blue-eyed Dutch. All of them were outnumbered by the flamboyant Frenchmen, many of them wearing huge moustaches that curled on either side of their swarthy faces. In several of their buttonholes flashed the red, white and blue ribbon of the Legion of Honour, an institution created by Napoleon and awarded, in limited numbers, mainly for bravery in the field. These warriors talked incessantly, exchanged sweeping bows and salutes, and to the wonderment of their rustic hosts, embraced and kissed one another in public. Several of these young adventurers, the sailors in particular, wore hooped earrings and possessed a natural charm that captured many a maiden's heart. Then there were the civilian prisoners, some of them accompanied by their wives and families, most of whom were captured at sea on voyages to or from the French colonies. Plantation owners, civil servants, merchants, government officials, all mingled with the assortment of military and naval personnel and were absorbed with them into the communities they were assigned to. Lastly there were the 'detinues' or detainees as we would call them now. In the main these prisoners were wealthy French civilians who were visiting Britain during the lull in the wars that was brought about by the Treaty of Amiens. When war was declared once more in 1803 all British visitors in France were rounded up and interned, whereupon the British government retaliated by taking the French visitors prisoner. These unfortunate people, probably suffered more personal hardship than their countrymen in arms who, in the main, accepted their fate as a result of the fortunes of war.

With the arrival of these vanquished but still proud people there developed a prosperity undreamed of by the market traders and shopkeepers in the towns they were sent to. The allowances they received, and in many cases the private funds forwarded to them by their families and friends in France, represented a spending power that benefited every kind of trade. After paying for their rent, the captive's need for meat and drink, bread, clothes, coffee, tobacco, etc. resulted in a considerable boost to the local economy. The number of prisoners residing in each town was usually between 150 and 300 and every parole prisoner had to sign a document promising to obey certain rules, before they were allowed 'On Parole.' Briefly, these were as follows:

1. To behave decently and abide by the laws of the Kingdom.
2. Not to correspond directly or indirectly with France.
3. All correspondence to be approved by the Commissioners or Agents.
4. To be permitted to walk or ride not more than one mile from the limits of the parole towns, and not to go outside the parish boundaries or turn left or right.
5. Not to enter any field or take a turning from any cross road, the penalty for so doing to be imprisonment.
6. Imprisonment for rioting or improper behaviour.
7. Not to try to escape.

The boundaries were usually marked by milestones (there are still a few in place, with the quaint words 'Miol Stone' or '1 Miol' inscribed thereon), but in some places prominent landmarks were used – the 'Honour

Oak' was one, another was Polson Bridge at Launceston.

There was provision too for protecting prisoners from residents who might insult or abuse them. Offenders were dealt with 'By Law' which usually meant a fine in the rare instances when the culprits were prosecuted

Prisoners' parole stone, Whistley Hill, Ashburton. PHOTO: Mrs Wendy Major.

(and abuses did occasionally take place). The official notices that were posted advising inhabitants of the parole rules sometimes prompted local misfits to act as spies and report any breaches of curfew in the hope of claiming the ten shillings reward offered for such information.

In 1796 those eligible for parole included boatswains, gunners, ships carpenters, master caulkers, and sail makers. These were practical men who most likely were responsible for carrying out various public works, some of which can be seen today, and which will be described later (by 1808 the list was limited and these categories were excluded). Great care had to be taken when selecting the parole towns because Britain was a refuge for large numbers of French Royalists, aristocrats and their families who had fled from Revolutionary France and were awaiting Napoleon's defeat before returning home to assume once more what they regarded as their rightful place in society. There were several clashes between them and soldiers of the Empire, and the authorities kept them apart whenever possible. In addition, nearly all parole towns were situated away from the coast so as to discourage escape attempts. As we shall presently see there were many escapes despite the prisoners giving their word of honour not to.

All prisoners of war, whether on the hulks (prison ships), the land depots, or living on parole, came under the jurisdiction of the Commissioners to the Transport Board (or Office), a department of the Admiralty. The Board appointed Agents to act on their behalf to ensure the rules drawn up for the care and supervision of prisoners were adhered to. On the prison ships and in the depots the Agents were invariably appointed from officers of the Royal Navy, but in the parole towns many of them were selected from among the professional men living there, surgeons and solicitors for example; shopkeepers and tradesmen were not eligible as it was considered necessary to employ 'men of quality' who

OFFICER RANKS ELIGIBLE FOR PAROLE IN 1808.

Of Men of War:
  Admirals.
  Chefs de Division, or Commodores.
  Captains. Lieutenants,
  Ensigns
  Aspirants (Midshipmen).
  Surgeons.
  Pursers.
  Secretaries.
  Chaplains and Schoolmasters.
Of the Land Service:
  Every officer bearing a Commission not lower than Sous-
  Lieutenant. Commissaries and Secretaries.
  Surgeons.
Of unarmed Merchant vessels of 80 tons and upwards:
  Masters.
  First Captains.
  Surgeons.
Of Privateers having 14 or more mounted Carriage Guns.
  Captains.
  Two other officers (according to Seniority) for every
  hundred men on board at time of capture.
  Surgeons.
All Passengers of Respectability, if detained; but those only are to
be considered as Passengers who are entered as such on the Role
de Equipage.
N.B. Prisoners taken in recaptured vessels are to be considered
according to their respective Ranks on board the Enemy's Vessels
to which they belong; and Officers of Merchant Vessels and
privateers are only to be considered as such, notwithstanding any
Rank they may hold in the Public Service of the Enemy.
  ☞ All prisoners of the Rank of Field Officer are to be allowed
  one servant each, but none other.

were able to deal effectively with the proud officers in their charge. Nevertheless it became the practice later to appoint all Agents exclusively from Royal Navy Lieutenants with at least ten years service.

Their duties included acting as intermediaries between the prisoners and the Transport Board, arranging the curfew times according to the time of year, holding a roll call twice a week when prisoners answered personally to their names, ensuring all the conditions for parole were obeyed and reporting breaches of parole, and paying them their subsistence allowances. Many officers came from prosperous families who were permitted to send them sums of money to supplement their subsistence pay. All payments were made through the Agents who were awarded the equivalent of 5% of all disbursements in addition to their salaries for undertaking these responsibilities. The Board recognised there were temptations and, in an age notorious for corruption and malpractice, often concealed under the guise of respectability, did all they could to eliminate such abuses as charging a 'commission' for paying the prisoners their dues. In fact the parole instructions to Agents specifically stated no 'commissions' were to be charged and in the rare instances where it occurred those responsible were made to refund any such money in addition to being reprimanded or removed from office.

All parole prisoners received a subsistence allowance from the British Government with which to pay for their food and lodgings. The allowance for senior officers was one shilling and sixpence per day, later increased to two shillings (the equivalent of 10p today) with a lower rate for the junior officers of one shilling and three pence, increased to one shilling and eight pence. There had been strong complaints from the Frenchmen, backed up by letters from the French Admiralty, claiming the allowances were inadequate owing to the greater expense of living in Britain. To their credit the Transport Board called upon a British officer who had recently escaped from France to furnish them with the latest prices in the French markets in order to compare them with those in this country. It then became clear the complaints were justified and the allowance was increased as already stated.

No allowance was payable for sick prisoners except for those with serious ailments, in which case the authorities arranged for doctors to attend. In general though, the sick were taken to the prisoner of war depots (of which Dartmoor Prison was one, Mill Prison in Plymouth another) for medical treatment. However there was an allowance for burying those who died, not to exceed two guineas, and it was stipulated plain coffins only were to be used. Many parole prisoners died and were buried in the

PAROLE DECLARATION WHICH WAS SIGNED BY ALL OFFICERS BEFORE GOING ON PAROLE.

(These varied slightly from time to time but the basic requirements remained unchanged)

'Whereas the Commissioners for conducting H.M.'s Transport Service and for the care and custody of French officers and sailors detained in England have been pleased to grant *name of prisoner* leave to reside in *name of town* upon condition that he gives his parole of honour not to withdraw one mile from the boundaries prescribed there without leave for that purpose from the said Commissioners, that he will behave himself decently and with due regard to the laws of the Kingdom, and also that he will not directly indirectly hold any correspondence with France during his continuance in England, but by such letters as shall be shown to the Agent of the said Commissioners under whose care he is or may be in order to them being read and approved by the Superiors, he does hereby declare that having given his parole he will keep it inviolably.'

OFFICIAL NOTICE POSTED IN THE PAROLE TOWNS ADVISING INHABITANTS HOW TO BEHAVE TOWARDS OFFICER PRISONERS.

'Notice is hereby given, that all such prisoners are permitted to walk or ride on the great turnpike road within the distance of one mile from the extreme parts of the town (not beyond the bounds of the parish) and that if they shall exceed such limits or go into any field or cross-road they may be taken up and sent to prison, and a reward of ten shillings will be paid by the Agent for apprehending them. And further, that such prisoners are to be in their lodgings by 5 o'clock in the winter, and 8 in the summer months, and if they stay out later they are liable to be taken up and sent to the Agent for such misconduct. And to prevent the prisoners from behaving in an improper manner to the inhabitants of the town, or creating any riots or disturbances either with them or among themselves, notice is also given that the Commissioners will cause, upon information being given to their Agents, any prisoners who shall so misbehave to be committed to prison. And such of the inhabitants who shall insult or abuse any of the Prisoners of War on parole, or shall be found in any respect aiding or assisting in the escape of such prisoners shall be punished according to law.'

From *Prisoners of War in Britain 1756–1815* (Francis Abell) by kind permission of Oxford University Press.

local churchyards, their names being recorded in the Parish records, together with their status ('a French prisoner' for example) often with the comment 'Buried in Linen According to Law'. The latter phrase refers to an Act of 1678 which stated:

'No corpse of any person (except those who die of the Plague) shall be buried in any shirt, shift, sheet, shroud, or anything whatsoever made or mingled with flax, hemp, silk, gold, hair, silver, or any stuff other than what is made from sheep's wool only… or to be put into any coffin lined or faced with any material but sheep's wool only'.

The Burial in Woollen Act was passed to protect and stimulate the wool trade, an essential part of our economy at that time and the Act was enforced up to 1814 with heavy penalties for failure to comply; hence Ministers and Parsons recorded the fact that this was done as a safeguard and the custom was extended to include prisoners of war. The Tavistock Parish records for the period mention only two deaths, those of an infant and a child, the names of whom are almost certainly French, although no mention is made of this or of the above Act. They are:

12th. Jan. 1805   Nicholas – Son of John Genelle   Aged 1
5th. Jan. 1806   Charles – Son of Charles Coniam   Aged 9

Once the parole prisoners had taken up residence, either in rented rooms or houses, or with local families, they were free to engage in any occupation or trade they desired as long as it was performed within the limit of their parole agreement. One officer is known to have opened a wine shop, whilst others who were accomplished in the arts taught music, dancing, drawing, and fencing. Many of them taught languages and were engaged as tutors for the children of well-to-do families.

There were other interesting developments. During the 18th. and 19th. centuries the English gentry, almost without exception, undertook what came to be called the 'Grand Tour' when, for periods of two or even three years, the sons of the rich and titled classes visited the Continent, staying for long periods in the cities of France and Italy in particular, these places being universally accepted as the centres of civilisation and culture. Armed with introductions to their counterparts, the young 'bucks' were sent to live there and acquire the attributes thought to be essential for a true 'English Gentleman'. They sought an appreciation of the arts – painting, literature, and music. Then there were languages and swordsmanship to be mastered, along with the courtly manners and refinements of the dining table and drawing room. When the wars broke out these excursions were no longer possible, but after a while it was realised they were not at all necessary because the very people who could teach them were on their doorstep so to speak – the army and naval officers on parole, most of whom, like themselves, were 'gentlemen of quality'. It should be remembered that after Napoleon became Emperor of the French he granted an amnesty to more than 40,000 Royalist *émigrés* living abroad enabling them to return home providing their future loyalty was to the Empire and to him. A great number of them were experienced officers who were needed for the army and navy of France. These men were much sought after by the local squires and dignitaries who welcomed them into their homes for their entertaining conversation and good manners to the extent (it was said) that the boundary stones previously mentioned were often moved by them to enable their guests to visit them whilst technically remaining within the one mile limit!

The craftsmen among the prisoners emulated their comrades in the prisons by manufacturing beautiful woodcarvings of ships and buildings, toys, and trinkets of all kinds to sell or barter for luxuries. The surgeons were permitted to set up in practice and several of them were repatriated as a gesture of gratitude for the good work they performed among the poor. In fact there are many instances where chivalrous deeds were rewarded by the repatriation of both French and British officers and more than one Frenchman was sent home to permit the release of a British prisoner, on condition neither of them took any further part in the war. An example of a very pleasant gesture of this kind was the release of a French seaman who leaped overboard from the 'Brave', one of the Plymouth based hulks, and saved the life of one Alexander Muir (confirmed in a letter dated 3rd. June 1810 from Captain Hawkins, the Agent). A French surgeon at Portsmouth was repatriated 'in consequence of his attention to sick soldiers on board the Transport ship 'Spence' (as represented by Lt. J.W. Lloyd of the 8th. King's Regiment'). As far as the populace were concerned (the upper classes especially, who enjoyed their lavish dinners and musical evenings as if it were peacetime) the wars were being fought so far away, often in remote parts of the world, they accepted their foreign 'guests' without rancour, and there was much goodwill extended both by them and the officer prisoners once they got to know one another.

Underlying all this was a thread of patriotism and loyalty to Napoleon which tried the patience of the Transport Board at times. Some French officers were allowed the privilege of having their wives join them from France, but this was discouraged and eventually banned after a series of escapes in which the women took an active part. One officer's wife came to England with the express intention of helping him to escape, bringing with her suitable clothing for a disguise. Her husband was General Lefebre Desnouettes who absconded from Cheltenham on 1st. May 1812 in the garb of a German count, assisted by his wife in male attire posing as his son. They were entirely successful and caused much embarrassment for the authorities, hence the ban on the entry of prisoner's wives to this country. During the course of the war (1803–1814) hundreds of officers broke their parole by escaping or 'running' as it was called, and from 5th June 1809 to 5th. June 1812 there were 440 escapes by officers on parole of whom only 242 were retaken. The British condemned them for dishonourable conduct, but many senior officer prisoners did not consider the parole rules binding on the grounds they were signed under duress, i.e. sign or go to prison, and perhaps they had a point.

Some escapes were vicious affairs where intervention by the citizens was resisted by force and murder ensued. There are examples of boat owners being threatened and compelled to take the runaways to France on pain of death, and on one occasion a group of officers on the run fought a battle with villagers who tried to apprehend them and stabbed one of them to death. Not all naval officers were captured on French men o'war, indeed the bulk of maritime prisoners in the early stages of the war were privateers men who were regarded by the British as little better than pirates, and in many cases that assertion would have been very close to the truth. As a result there was an element of officer ruffians at large who required a firm hand and had to be carefully watched.

There were women and girls in some of the towns most of whom were captured at sea, wives and children of ship's passengers mainly. As a rule they were billeted with families until the Transport Board decided what to do with them. Their decision was based on their status and nationality, but in the main they were repatriated and in any case it was stipulated they were not to be treated as prisoners. There are innumerable instances where wives elected to remain with their husbands, whether their husbands were civilians or officers, and whilst none were detained in the depots, there are records of a small number of females being detained on the hulks, presumably after choosing to accompany their husbands who may have been sent there for bad behaviour; some of these women must have been 'camp followers' or married to other ranks and were captured with them. In any case the Agents were required to supply them with victuals on request. Hence we learn that 'the French woman at Tavistock requests that Sir Rupert George (Chairman of the Transport Board) will interest himself to procure rations for her and her child, who was born at the Depot and is nearly five months old'. This she was perfectly entitled to do and this type of petition was not unusual. By 'the Depot' she almost certainly meant Prince Town and not the prison there.

Number of Prisoners in 1812.

The Transport Board figures for the year 1812 show a total of 52,649 French prisoners in Britain of which 24,567 were army personnel, and 26,525 were sailors. In addition there were 1,557 'Others' – ship's passengers and the like, as previously mentioned.

The number of French Commissioned Officers on parole on 5th. June 1812 numbered 2,142 and there were besides: 211 'Passengers and other Persons of respectability', 115 women and children, and 149 servants to officers. There were 1,868 Danish captives, of whom 33 officers and 3 officer's servants were on parole (most of the lower ranks being held aboard the hulks at Plymouth).

ESCAPES

There were more than twice as many escapes by prisoners on parole for the year ending 5th June 1812 than in any one of the previous three years. As a result of the Duke of Wellington's successful Peninsular campaign, the number of prisoners taken by the British had increased dramatically and possibly this affected the escape figures. Since 5th June 1810 a total of 307 French Commissioned Officers had absconded – out of which only 157 were recaptured. From the Transport Office official report:

No. of escapes by Commissioned Officers for year ending 5th. June 1810 104
No. of escapes by Commissioned Officers for year ending 5th. June 1811 118
No. of escapes by Commissioned Officers for year ending 5th. June 1812 242

Total 464
No. recaptured 157
No. of successful escapes by officers 307

During the same 3 year period no less than 218 'others' escaped out of which only 85 were recaptured.

Several British women married French officers (and some took Danish and Dutch husbands). Association between the sexes was inevitable but the men on parole were discouraged from such liaisons and for good reason: the marriages that occurred were not recognised in France. In Tavistock it was recorded that 'some of the French officers had made overtures of marriage to women in the neighbourhood which the magistrates very properly have taken pains to discourage'. All the same very many marriages did take place, not only in the westcountry but all over Britain, and the Parish Registers bear witness to them. There were other relationships too, agreed temporary affiliations, or where marriage was out of the question for some reason. The result was there were a number of illegitimate children for whom the prisoners responsible had to pay maintenance, usually in the form of a lump sum. Failure to do so was punishable by terms of imprisonment.

A great deal of reliable information concerning French prisoners of war can be found in the archives of the Freemasons. Many French and British Regiments, and naval warships too, had established Lodges and more were set up in captivity, not only in the parole towns but on the hulks and in some war prisons (readers may be surprised to learn there were French Lodges established within Dartmoor prison and Mill prison in Plymouth). When the war finally ended the prisoners took the records of their meetings home, to be deposited in Lodges all over France, where they were found years later by British and French researchers and the contents made known. Many more are yet to be discovered but those uncovered so far provide invaluable documentary evidence of this important social aspect of their lives during captivity during which there were occasions when French parole prisoners were welcomed as visitors to some British Lodges, and several British citizens were admitted to the prisoner's Lodges, some of whom were made honourary members. Examples are given in the individual texts for the Dartmoor area parole towns, and it will be seen that in one or two cases the movements of certain officer prisoners can be traced which might not otherwise be possible because of lost or incomplete official records.

Much of what has been written so far might give the impression the officers who took parole had a cosy time. Nothing could be further from the truth. They were enemy captives living 'freely' by consent of the Transport Board, subject to strict rules which had to be obeyed, and the records often illustrate the fact they were never to assume their status was anything other than prisoners. For example, in a letter dated 28th Feb.

1814 to Mr. Gribble, the Ashburton Agent, the Board advised him that if any prisoner were to be found outside his lodgings after curfew 'he will immediately be ordered into close confinement'. In another letter the following month Mr. Gribble is told prisoners cannot be permitted to remain in one house whilst lodging in another after 'the time fixed for the bell-ringing' (a reference to curfew time) and that 'they are of course liable to be apprehended if found *out of their lodgings* after that time (author's italics). The implication is clear: simply being off the streets at curfew time was not good enough – prisoners had to be at their place of residence. Even when freedom was at hand the restraining hand of authority hovered over them. An extract from another communication to Mr. Gribble dated 20th. March 1815 (when the repatriation of the Americans was imminent) reads

'...In the event of your receiving orders for the release of any Prisoners who may be represented to be in Debt, you are to withhold the discharge of such Prisoners until the Creditors are satisfied or they shall have time to take the necessary measures for enforcing Payment of the Claims'.

Although the parole towns accommodated many hundreds of soldiers and sailors, often of mixed nationalities, little trace remains to mark their stay and in many instances the inhabitants today have not an inkling of their colourful past. There can be no doubt the young and adventurous Frenchmen and others created an unprecedented stir when they arrived in the quiet rural areas to which they were sent. The friendships they formed, and their acceptance into every kind of social activity, left a sad gap on their departure. In many cases the population turned out to cheer them on their way when they left for home, and of course the tradesmen missed the extra business they had engendered. Yet by the end of the 1800s the Ashburton Agent's descendants, for example, who still lived in the house in West Street where he used to preside over his charges, had no recollections, anecdotes, or mementoes of any kind to offer an enquirer who sought information about those turbulent days. It is hoped the following chapters may help to redress this gap in our history.

ASHBURTON – SIXTY YEARS ON PAROLE

This little market town, nestling on the edge of Dartmoor, was for more than sixty years the most well known and important of the parole towns. The prisoners on parole included not only the French and their allies, but American officers too. The latter were quartered exclusively either at Ashburton or Reading and were mostly navy personnel, both U.S.Navy men and Privateers' men. Official records are sparse but the reputation they left behind on their departure was a livelier one than that of the officers of other nations who shared their captivity here. It should be remembered though that at the commencement of hostilities all American seamen who happened to be in British ports at the time were taken captive. In addition, there were hundreds of Americans serving in British warships, most of whom declared their unwillingness to fight against their own country and elected to go as prisoners of war. Most of these men had seen active service against the French but were often treated with contempt by the very shipmates and officers they had sailed with for years. Some were whipped at the gangway as they left their ships with the words 'scoundrels' and 'rebels' ringing in their ears. The result, as you might expect, was a backlash of resentment and anger which caused endless trouble for the British in charge of the War Depots like Dartmoor and at Ashburton from the officers on parole.

During the Napoleonic War 1803–1814 the Agent was Mr. Joseph Gribble, a local solicitor, who lived at No. 42 West Street. The lovely old house can still be seen opposite the Old Vicarage and is remarkably well preserved. The parole prisoners were required to muster outside the house every Tuesday and Saturday at 10.00 a.m. when every man personally answered to his name. Mr. Gribble allocated their lodgings and drew up the curfew times which were:

Not permitted outside before 6.00 a.m.

To be in residence by 6.00 p.m. November, December, and January.

7.00 p.m. February, March, April, September, and October,

9.00 p.m. May, June, July, and August.

There was a Guard House (remembered locally as the 'lock up') for the confinement of malcontents a little further up the hill from Mr. Gribble's residence at what is now No.2 and No. 3 Bowden Hill. In those days it was a grim, stone built block with heavily barred windows, quite unlike the two pleasant converted dwellings which are there now. Mention has already

*The old prison (known as
the lock-up) Bowden Hill,
Ashburton.*
Reproduced by kind permission of
Ashburton Museum

*Mr Gribble's house, West Street,
Ashburton.*

been made of the form of parole which every officer was required to sign, and an example of one such document is shown opposite. The original document was acquired by a visitor to France who presented a copy to Ashburton Museum. The translation confirms the conditions of parole.

There used to be a total of eight milestones on the roads leading out of the town, marking the limits to which the prisoners could go from the town centre. Local people refer to them as 'Parole Stones', and seven of them are known to exist now, although their exact locations have not been revealed for security reasons. (One of the stones went missing and was discovered in someone's private garden; fortunately the matter was settled amicably and it was replaced in its original location). The best known one lies at the side of the Broadhampstead road by a sharp bend and it is said the Frenchmen moved this stone further along and around the corner to enable them to enjoy an enhanced view! Sadly, a number of 'miol stones' all over Britain were defaced or destroyed by over zealous officials in 1940 when, in the face of a possible enemy invasion, an Act was passed whereby signposts and other directional signs which might be useful to invading forces had to be removed.

Prisoners who didn't go home.

A Dutchman, some Danes, and at least two Americans were buried in Ashburton's churchyard. The Parish Registers record the following:

Gerand Witmont, a Dutch prisoner...   died...4th. June 1782.

Peter Nessam, a Danish prisoner...   died...6th. October 1808

Christianna Holback (daughter of Peter, a Danish Captain)...
        died...13th. November 1808

Sophic Hanson (daughter of Peter, a Dane)...
        died...11th. October 1811
    (the ages of the above are not recorded)

Benjamin Elweel, American prisoner on parole...
        died...12th. March 1815
    Aged 35. Buried by Mr. Lowndes, Minister.

Abraham Burnham, American prisoner on parole...
        died...20th. March 1815
    Aged 30. Burial carried out by Mr. Huxham, Minister.

FRENCH PRISONERS OF WAR IN GREAT BRITAIN

Monsieur GILLET has produced a copy of the rules to be observed by prisoners of war in Great Britain. On the reverse side of the document there are the following instructions:

The days to report are Tuesdays and Saturdays at my office at ten in the morning. All mail you wish to be delivered must be sent weekly on Saturday.

When lodgings are obtained this must be reported to me and do not change them without my permission.

RULES WHICH ALL PRISONERS OF WAR ON PAROLE MUST OBSERVE

The prisoner given Parole of Honour will not leave the prescribed bounds without having obtained permission to this effect from the Commissioners responsible for Prisoners of War.

He will conduct himself with decency and with due regard to the laws of Great Britain and Ireland and moreover, during his stay in England, he will not enter into any correspondence directly or indirectly with an enemy of His Britannic Majesty. He will not receive or send any letter or letters by the hand of the Agent to the said Commissioners which may not be read or approved by him.

The following are the prescribed limits:

The prisoner is allowed to walk within one mile of the town centre but he must not enter open land or road, nor be absent from his lodgings after 5 p.m. November, December, January; after 7 p.m. in February, March, September or October; After 9 p.m. June and July, and he must not leave his lodgings before 6 a.m.

Both the Americans were in fact free men and not prisoners when they died. The Treaty of Ghent which terminated the War of 1812 had been signed on Christmas Eve 1814, was ratified in the USA in February 1815, and therefore they would have been waiting for transport to take them home. We do not know exactly where they lie, but the term 'Minister' suggests the burials were Nonconformist as might be expected in their case.

Several Frenchmen died and were buried here. Prior to 1800 only two names are recorded, the others simply have the entry: 'A French Prisoner of War' and the dates. The two whose names are known are: Jacques Leguby (Lt. from Man O' War 'Gentille')...

died...12th. June 1796.

Foussant Gatel (a Planter from Martinique)...

died...14th. October 1796.

The only prisoner of war in Ashburton known to have had a headstone was Francois Guidon, a soldier. The stone is still there, to the right of the main entrance to the church, on a little mound which used to be called 'Stranger's Hill' on account of the unfortunate Francois being the only person buried in that part of the churchyard, and a foreigner. Today he shares the Hill with Ashburton folk who died later, but his grave is instantly recognisable because there is a willow tree growing behind it. This tree is said to have grown from a shoot taken from a willow near Napoleon's grave on St. Helena. The sceptics among us would say this was unlikely, but the facts suggest otherwise. Napoleon himself chose his last resting place on the island, in the Vale of Geranium, afterwards named the Valley of the Tomb. The tomb was close by 'Torbett's Spring' where the Emperor's drinking water was taken from and which was surrounded by willow trees. His funeral was attended by hundreds of British army officers and men who had guarded him, and a number of French officers who had elected to follow him into exile. After the ceremony nearly everyone broke off sprigs of willow and even small branches as souvenirs of the occasion, stripping the trees almost bare in the process. Later still, when the British forces withdrew from the island, a sergeant who had married a local girl was permitted to remain, and was appointed guardian of the tomb. Being an enterprising fellow, he cultivated some ground in order to grow willow shoots which he sold to visitors from passing ships, but only after they had rooted in old wine bottles filled with spring water and sealed. It is known that several of these shoots were brought back to Europe intact, making the tale relating to Lt. Guidon's grave a very likely one, in which case a shoot could have been planted there by friends or relatives. The inscription on his headstone reads:

Ici

Repose Francois Guidon
Matif de Cambrai en France
Sous Lieutenant au 16th. Reg.
de Lign. Decede le 18 7bre
1815 age 22 ans.
Recquisat in Pace.

The official Entry Book gives the date of his death as 18/12/1815. Other accounts interpret the date as 18th. July 1815. Whichever is correct, young Guidon died after Napoleon's final defeat at the Battle of Waterloo, and when freedom was at hand. The wording on the headstone was re-cut in 1903 and a photograph of it was sent to the Mayor of Cambrai. He wrote to say no family of that name could be traced and that the photograph and details had been forwarded to the President of the Committee of the Society for the Preservation of French Soldier's Graves in France and Abroad.

The most celebrated of Ashburton's 'guests' was undoubtedly General Count Etienne Pierre Cambronne who commanded the First Chasseurs of the Old Guard (the French Imperial Guard, one of the elite units of the French army) at the Battle of Waterloo. In the final phase of that battle the Guards were surrounded and, having fought bravely, were invited by the British to surrender with honour. The general himself answered: "The Guard dies, it does not surrender!" (he is also credited with having answered with one short word – and a very rude one at that). General Cambronne was close to the Emperor Napoleon all through the wars, more a friend than a subordinate commander, and had rejoined him after his escape from Elba in 1815. He was badly wounded in the battle and was left for dead on the field when he was found and shipped to England. One account states that the General became separated from his men and was captured single-handedly by an officer of the German Legion who dragged him to the British lines. He was sent first to the Portsmouth hulks, but as soon as his identity became known he was transferred to Ashburton on parole. During his stay a local doctor treated his wounds, but the General carried the scars of battle on his forehead for the rest of his life. His home was with Mrs. Eddy, wife of Sergeant Eddy of the Ashburton Sergebacks (believed to have been a Volunteer Force), who lived in a little house in the High Street opposite Station Road (now named Lawrence Lane). He must have received kind attention from Mrs. Eddy during his short stay because on his departure for France in November 1815 he gave her, as a mark of gratitude, a fine portrait of himself, of which she was very proud. In time the picture passed to her daughter, Mrs. Clymo, whose husband James Clymo was landlord

French Lt. Guidon's grave in Ashburton churchyard. *French Lt. Guidon's headstone.*

of the Golden Lion Hotel in Ashburton from 1901 to 1910. This was the finest inn in the town and the portrait remained on display there for several years. Today its whereabouts is unknown – a charming relic of the past has vanished (descendants of the Clymo family: search your attics, you may find a priceless reminder of the Frenchmen's stay in your town).

The Parish Marriage Records reveal the names of several Militiamen and Regular soldiers who married into the community (Ashburton was also a Garrison town), as well as the French who also made successful overtures:

April 1797   Liasente Cupeance married Ann Croad
May 1797   Louis Bruisquet married Johanna King
Among the Baptisms are:
17 April 1797   Blad, John, S.of Jean (a French prisoner) and
                   Ann Croad.
16 August 1797   George Croad. Base child of Ann.

There is a mystery here. Was George Croad the child of Ann who was married in April that year? If so, what happened to her husband and why is the child labelled 'Base?'.

As we have seen, in every Parole town there were love affairs (and some marriages) that ended suddenly when the prisoners were repatriated. Many a young lady was betrayed by a lover or husband among the prisoners, some of whom already had wives at home. Benjamin Palmer, an American sailor released from Dartmoor prison in 1815, wrote about his embarkation at Plymouth with bitterness and resentment after seeing men ordered off the ship that was to take them home to make room for a number of officers who had been at Ashburton on parole. With drink flowing freely there was soon trouble and fights broke out between the Dartmoor prisoners and the parole men. Palmer's final comment is contemptuous of the 'Ashburton Gentry' as he called them, 'most of whom has made the girls sorry they ever saw them.' We can only surmise what the implications were in this remark, but there were at least two happier and honourable conclusions to such affairs.

From the Parish Registers we learn that on 16 January 1815 William Miller, 'an American on parole' and a bachelor, married Mary Harding, spinster, by Licence and with the consent of her parents. The War of 1812 ended on Christmas Eve 1814 when the Treaty of Ghent was signed by representatives of Britain and the United States, and although the ratification of the Treaty by the United States Government had not yet been received, William Miller and his comrades would have been looking forward to their release. This, together with the Licence factor, suggests there was some urgency, but whether or not we assume Mary Harding was expecting his child (in which case the law would have compelled William to accept his responsibility) he evidently had the approval of her parents and married her.

A more interesting case, and a romantic one, involved Midshipman William Pottenger, 'an American prisoner on parole' who was married to Frances Broom, spinster, on 21 November 1814, with the consent of her mother. He was one of a group of officers from the United States Brig 'Argus', captured after a sea battle with His Majesty's Brig 'Pelican' off the coast of Ireland in August 1814. It was a notable engagement because it was the first time a United States Navy crew were taken prisoner during the war with America (those Americans already in captivity were mainly merchant seamen, ex-Royal Navy sailors who refused to fight against their country, or privateersmen). The 'Argus' had captured or sunk several British merchant ships, and her defeat was regarded as a triumph for the Royal Navy. More significantly with regard to our story, the United States Government wanted the crew repatriated on exchange as soon as possible, their navy being short of experienced men. Consequently, in October 1814, after being given priority over all other prisoners in England, the officers and crew of the 'Argus' were sent to Dartmouth to embark on Cartels for home, with the exception of one man – Midshipman Pottenger. He was in trouble and was being held in custody by the Ashburton Magistrates probably in the 'lock-up'. In a letter of 9th. November 1814 from the Transport Office to the Ashburton Agent, Mr. Joseph Gribble, we learn that:

'no Allowance can be made to Mr.Pottenger while he remains in the Custody of the Civil Power, but if he should be liberated by the Magistrates before any opportunity offers for his returning to the United States, he will again be admitted to Parole'.

This tells us William Pottenger had not broken the terms of his parole or committed any civil offence, because if he had, he would have been sent either to Dartmoor or Mill Prison in Plymouth in the first instance, or brought before the Civil Courts in the second. In fact neither happened – he was married twelve days later, and we may assume that (as in the case of William Miller before him) a young woman's reputation was at stake, something that was taken very seriously in those days. Mr. Ira Dye of California, and formerly of the University of Virginia, an author and authority on the events of that time concerning United States sailors and their captivity in England, has confirmed Midshipman Pottenger returned to his home in Philadelphia on 1st. August 1815 and that a few months later he went back to Ashburton and brought Frances Broom (the first 'G.I. bride'?) home. Consider what that journey must have entailed: first a trek (probably on horseback or by coach) to the nearest seaport; a voyage by sailing ship perhaps of several weeks duration, with all the hazards associated with transatlantic travel in those days; then another land journey to Ashburton. Finally, William Pottenger returned home with Frances, completing his second round trip in less than a year. That surely was an act of true love.

Mr. Dye told the author that Frances Pottenger outlived her husband by several years, and spent the rest of her life in the United States, being in receipt of a United States Navy pension. There is no record of any offspring however.

Finally, there was Lieut. Uriah P. Levy (another 'Argus' officer) among the Americans at Ashburton. The French may have gloried over General Cambronne, but Lieut. Levy was destined to become one of the most celebrated officers in the United States Navy and is best remembered as the man who was instrumental in abolishing flogging (it ceased in 1862, the year of his death). When in command aboard ship he preferred to punish wrongdoers by other, unofficial and unorthodox methods which landed him in trouble with his superiors. He himself suffered humiliation and prejudice from certain of his fellow officers because of his Jewish origins and the fact he entered the navy as a Lieutenant straight from the merchant service instead of the conventional route of Midshipman. Altogether he survived no less than six courts martial, being completely exonerated each time on appeal. Despite these setbacks, he rose through the ranks and in 1858 was promoted to Commodore of the Mediterranean Fleet, the United States Navy's highest post at that time and equivalent to Admiral. He is remembered now not only as an officer of outstanding ability, but a clever investor who used much of his accumulated wealth to restore President Thomas Jefferson's home, which had fallen into a state of disrepair. He also commissioned a statue of that great man which he presented to the United States government, and which was installed in the rotunda of the United States Capitol building where it can be seen today. A grateful (and perhaps penitent) nation named a World War II destroyer 'USS Levy' in his honour and the United States Navy's Jewish Chapel at Norfolk, Virginia is named Commodore Levy Chapel.

Altogether an impressive record for a former prisoner of war on parole at Ashburton.

MORETONHAMPSTEAD.

The first French officer came to Moretonhampstead on parole on 23rd. January 1807. A month later he was in trouble for breaking one of the conditions of his parole, and so was farmer Samuel Potter who was summoned before Mr. Justice Roberts at Drewsteignton to be reprimanded for helping him do it. He had taken the Frenchman to see his farm, which entailed leaving the highway – a breach of the parole rules. Mr. Potter was lucky in that on this occasion no further punishment was awarded. The first Spanish officer arrived on 22nd. February that same year, and on 29th. August seven more arrived, one of them a General. The Danes started to arrive on January 7th. 1808. During the next five years the town became a truly international community.

The citizens of the town beheld an amazing sight when, on 17th. October 1809, a coloured man known as Peter the Black married a local girl, Susanna Parker. The groom's real name was Pierre Courpon who was captured at sea off the French possession of San Domingo (now the Republic of Haiti) with his master General Jean Baptiste Donatien de Vimeur, Count de Rochambeau, whose servant he was. Both men were on parole at Moretonhampstead from July 1807 to March 1811. We are told 'the novelty of the occasion and the popularity of the happy pair was reflected in the great throng of people who assembled at the church and paraded with them down the street to a joyous peal of bells which rang nearly all that day'.

The little Dartmoor town played host to a total of 379 prisoners during the war; there were 250 there in the year 1811 alone, most of whom were French and among whom General de Rochambeau was the most famous and notorious. He was one of Napoleon's ablest generals and a hero to the French, but to the British he was an endless source of annoyance in captivity and had to be transferred more than once before finally settling in Moretonhampsted. He was there for three and a half years before being exchanged and repatriated, together with his servant. The last we hear about Mrs. Courpon was five months after her husband's departure, when their son John Peter (born 26th. August 1811) was Christened by Nonconformist Minister Theo. Edwards on 1st. September that same year.

Moretonhampstead owes a great debt to Mr. Sylvester Treleaven who was at that time a postmaster, chemist, and bookseller in the town and whose shop was near the corner where the road goes to Chagford, known locally as 'Treleaven's Corner'. He took a lively interest in daily events and recorded them from 1799 onwards in a book entitled *Chronological Occurrences at Moreton*, generally referred to today as 'Treleavens Diary'.

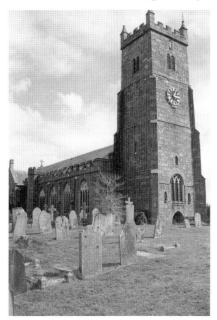

The parish church of St Andrew, Moretonhampstead.

The site of the cross tree at Moretonhampstead.

In it he gives us an insight into the activities of the officers on parole, many of them eyewitness accounts. Thus we learn the details of the wedding of General Rochambeau's servant as well as other pleasing events. For example in 1807, on 15th. August (Napoleon's birthday) 'the Frenchmen celebrated with great festivity but in a manner as not to give offence to the inhabitants'. Four days later they performed with their band of music at the famous Cross Tree 'and played several airs with great taste and precision'. The good relationships which obviously existed between them and the citizens of Moreton were further enhanced on 4th. February 1808 when a serious fire broke out. It started at the 'Dolphin Hotel', which was owned by a Mr. Tozer, and it very quickly spread, threatening to engulf the town. The Moreton Volunteers, a local Militia unit, turned out to help under the direction of their Commanding Officer, John Ponsford, a Surgeon in the town who also acted as Agent to the prisoners on parole. Labourers in the fields saw the flames and ran to help, finding themselves joined by the French and Danish officers. Over 1500 men of various nationalities, friend and foe, toiled side by side carrying water for the pumps and removing furniture to safety. The 'Dolphin' was destroyed, but the town was saved. At a meeting that night at the 'White Hart' the gentlemen of the town proposed a public vote of thanks to the prisoners on parole for their help; the labourers and poor folk did rather better, being treated to a handsome dinner paid for by public subscription.

On 17th. May 1808 the Moreton Volunteers paraded to be inspected by Captain Fulford of the West Devon Militia. He was also a Magistrate and the occasion afforded an opportunity to investigate an assertion that General Rochambeau had in his possession 'certain papers or charts inimical to this government'. Captain Ponsford, accompanied by the Militia sergeants, marched to the General's house and interrogated him, but he denied everything and as a search revealed nothing the matter was dropped. The general was a defiant, brave man, who made a point of wearing his full dress uniform complete with medals and decorations whenever there was news of a French victory. These occasions were deliberate acts of provocation because the general was known to scorn military honours and had refused to accept what is today France's highest decoration, the Legion of Honour, instituted by Napoleon himself. There were many like him among the prisoners in Britain whose love of France and dedication to their Emperor, together with an unflinching fighting spirit, was long remembered after their departure (and secretly admired by many who had charge of them). General de Rochambeau was killed at Leipzig in October 1813 in a great battle that lasted three days, afterwards called the 'Battle of the Nations'.

The circumstances under which the General and his men were captured are interesting and help explain his unrelenting hostility towards the British. In 1802, during the Peace of Amiens, there was a slave revolt on the island of San Domingo in the West Indies, and an expedition twenty thousand strong was sent to pacify the island under the overall command of General Victoire Emmanuel Leclerc, Napoleon's brother-in-law, with Rochambeau as his army commander. It was a disaster. The rebel troops, led by their black General Jean-Jacques Dessalines, formerly an officer in the French army, were not only familiar with the terrain but immune to diseases like Yellow Fever and Malaria which killed the French in thousands, including their General Leclerc. Within six months General de Rochambeau, his army decimated by death in battle and from disease, was forced to surrender and was given permission for his men and all their baggage to sail for France – generous terms indeed and he must have been well pleased. Then came the ultimate humiliation, because, unknown to them, the Treaty of Amiens had ended and war had broken out again. A British fleet appeared off the coast of San Domingo and the General and the surviving remnants of his army were captured. They were detained first at Jamaica from whence they were transferred to England, arriving in September 1804. General de Rochambeau was outraged and never forgave his enemy for what he considered a breach of convention in taking his men prisoner in such a manner.

At Moretonhampstead the French, who were renowned for their musical talents and theatricals, had rivals in the field of entertainment, for on 20th. October 1808 the Dutch and Danish officers there were allocated a portion of Mrs. Harvey's malt house which they converted to a theatre, completing the work in under a month 'in a very competent manner'.

The Dutch were rivals on the field of love too, as the following excerpts from the records reveal:

10th. March 1811. Johannes Schindehutte married Elizabeth Parker. (we do not know if she was related to Susanna who married Peter the Black). In the General Entry Book kept by the Agent his name is written as Lt.Johan Schendehutte captured on board the Indiaman 'Gode Thou'.

Raymond Domingo, a French naval officer married Elizabeth Scott, probably on the same day. His name was recorded by the Agent as Capt. Rai Dominigo of the Privateer ship 'Rodour'.

Banns were recorded for the intended marriage of Frederic Francois Senecal (French) and Eliza Sarah Edwards, but there is no record of the marriage taking place. He is named as Sous Lt. F.F. le Senecal in the Entry Book, a soldier of the 66th. Infantry Regiment, and a passenger on a captured merchant ship.

At least three French officers died in Moreton and were buried in the churchyard. Their headstones once stood among the other graves, but two of them are now mounted on the wall of the entrance porch to the church, and the third has disappeared. Here are the details:

'A LA MEMOIRE DE
JEAN FRANCOIS ROHAN
ASPIRANT DE LA MARINE IMPERIALE
AGE 21 ANS. DECIDE LE 22 JANVIER 1811.'
(Aspirant = Cadet or Midshipman).

The stone bore the emblem of sword and anchor crossed, and his is the missing stone. Young Rohan was a passenger on the 'Maria Louisa', a merchant ship, and was a prisoner for only five months when he died. The other two headstones are illustrated. Lt. Quantin's has a Masonic symbol under the inscription, and although it has been suggested this could have been a Regimental emblem, he was buried with full Masonic honours. He was evidently a popular man because 104 French and Danish officers attended the funeral as well as 'most of the respectable residents of the town' (Treleaven's Diary). Sadly his Passport for Exchange arrived just 24 hours before his death which was, incidentally, the first among the officers on parole there. Lt. Aubry was a veteran of several campaigns and rose to officer rank from that of a common soldier. He had been a prisoner before in 1791. In 1809 he was promoted to Full Lieutenant only to be taken prisoner again in the Peninsula the following year. It was to be his last campaign.

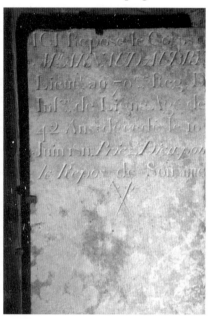

Lt. Quantin's headstone.
The inscription reads:

A LA MEMOIRE DE LOUIS
AMBROISE QUANTIN LIEUT. DU 144
REGT. DU CORPS IMPERIALE
D'ARTILLERIE DE MARINE.
AGE DE 33 ANS
DECEDE LE 29 D'AVRIL 1810.

Lt. Aubry's headstone
The inscription reads:

ICI REPOSE LE CORPS DE M.
ARNAUD AUBRY LIEUT. AU 70 REGT.
DE LIGNE.
AGE DE 42 ANS. DECEDE LE 10 JUIN
1811. PRIEZ DIEU POR LE REPOSE DE
SON AME.
PHOTO: Ian Snell

Several officers absconded from Moretonhampstead and one occurrence is worthy of attention because it involved five French officers. They were: Louis Hamel, Captain (merchant ship), Allain Michel, 2nd. Captain (merchant ship), Pierre Joseph Denis, 2nd. Captain (privateer), Casimer Baudouin, Lt. (merchant ship), Andre Fleuriot, Midshipman (merchant ship).

A 'carrier' called Richard Tapper met them on the night of 26th January 1811, provided them with horses, and guided them to Topsham where they boarded a vessel belonging to Thomas and William Vinnicombe, who came from Cheriton Bishop and were professional smugglers. For a down payment of £25 and the promise of a further £250 on arrival, they had agreed to take the fugitives to France. The venture ended in failure when they ran aground in the estuary of the River Exe and were apprehended. According to Mr. Treleaven's diary the Frenchmen were brought back to Moretonhampstead where they were guarded by the Militia before being taken to Drewsteignton to appear in front of Mr. Justice Roberts who committed then to 'high gaol'. At the Devon Summer Assize the following year, Tapper and the two Vinnicombe brothers were sentenced to transportation for life. The French officers were sent to Mill Prison at Plymouth to be imprisoned there for the duration of the war.

Our glimpse of Moretonhampstead concludes with a happier story. One of the many young men who won the heart of a local maiden was 24 year old Ensign de Vasseau Jean George Rihl, who was captured on the French man o' war 'La Basque' in November 1809. He was sent first to North Tawton and transferred to Moreton on 22nd. March 1810 where he stayed nearly two years. During that time he met and loved a girl called Ann Soper, and the result of their union was the birth of a son, William, who grew up to be a watchmaker of considerable skill. It was he who substituted the letters of his name for the numbers on the face of a special clock he made, and finding he was one letter short, added an extra 'L', which is how the family name of Rihll was established. One of his direct descendants, the late Mr. Harry Rihll of Moretonhampstead, was a popular local Councillor. He also owned two chemist shops, one in Moreton, the other in Chagford, and became a celebrity when he formulated 'Rihll's Real Rennet – for Devon's Dainty Dish', a reference to Devonshire junkets (of Miss Muffet fame) of which Rennet is an essential ingredient. Mr. George Friend, who was a close friend and associate of his for over 40 years, told the author Mr. Rihll's brown hair, blue eyes, and strongly rounded features were unmistakably like those of his romantic ancestor whose background he had researched.

OKEHAMPTON AND NORTH TAWTON.

'HIC V...T FUIT CAPTIVUS BELLI' (here V...t was a prisoner of war). These words were cut into a stone in Okehampton castle by a French prisoner on parole in 1809 and can still be traced, although the stone (a small tablet on the wall of the Pascina) has been defaced by other, more recent graffiti. Who was V...t? A highly respected local historian of long ago, the late Dr.E.H.Young, identified him as Gilles Vincent, Surgeon on the French man o'war 'La Rejoirie', who was captured on 10th. June 1809, and a study of the Public Record Office list of prisoners of war on parole in Okehampton during the Napoleonic War confirms this. Vincent was one out of a total of 336 prisoners who were sent to the town between 15th. May 1809 and 27th. February 1812. There were 162 French navy men, 131 army personnel, 31 ship's passengers, 3 ship's boys, 6 wives and 3 children.

Okehampton Castle

This was not the first time French prisoners were on parole in Okehampton. They were there in 1758 during the Seven Years War when, as the Parish Records reveal, two marriages and two baptisms took place. On 18th.July that year Jacque Gohet Duchaine (Mariner) married Mary Rowe and their daughter, Frances, was baptised on 19th. November the same year. In March 1762 another daughter, Mary, was baptised. On 20th. November 1758 Jean Francois Busquet, 'a Prisoner on Parole and Barber Surgeon', married Honor Woodman and their son, Charles, was baptised on 21st. January 1759. The name of Busquet survives in the Westcountry as Busket or Buskett, and is but one example of the legacy the Frenchmen left behind when they went home.

To return to the year 1809, when Okehampton was but a wayside halt on the Launceston–Tavistock–Exeter road, the influx of French officers and civilians, must have caused an immense upheaval. For the prisoners, who had led exciting and active lives, the place must have been intolerable at first with just one main street amidst the sleepy countryside of mid-Devon and their frustration probably contributed to an outbreak of riotous behaviour and fighting which broke out one day, when they were dispersed single-handed by Doctor Luxmoore, a fine big chap on a fine big horse, who rode into the fray with riding whip in hand. The Luxmoores were a prominent Okehampton family who for many years occupied the lovely old house in Fore Street now used by Okehampton Borough council.

The prisoner's mess room is recorded as having been situated in the Old Schoolroom in St. James's Street opposite the entrance to the present arcade, and was probably for the use of ordinary soldiers and sailors who were servants to senior officers. The building was demolished many years ago. Not surprisingly among so many seafarers, they soon settled down and established a reputation for model making, mainly toys, cribbage boards, etc. and buildings – especially churches. They are also credited with having laid the cobbled pathways in Okehampton Parish churchyard. This must have been the work of the lower ranks, and although the charge might be made that the French prisoners apparently spent all their waking hours laying cobbled paths in churchyards etc., the reader can make a judgement on the basis that the paths are there, they are very old, and local traditions more often than not have a grain of truth in them concerning more unlikely events than these.

As was the case in every parole town, the younger men enjoyed relationships with local girls, and some of these became permanent, as the Marriage Registers reveal:

3rd. May 1810	Nicolai Leonard to Julia Hamden Brock (Licence).
24th. December 1810	Charles Pie to Elizabeth Middlewick.
27th. December 1810	Louis de Lettre to Emma Jole (Licence).
11th January 1811	Felix Jean Ricard to Mary Quick, a Sojourner (Licence).
8th December 1811	Louis Alexandre Huet (of Caen in Normandy) to Jane Seldon (Licence).

All the Frenchmen except Huet, are described as 'a prisoner of war'. He was a merchant, a passenger on the French man o' war 'La Mouche' when he was captured. Like a great many prisoners, he elected to remain in England with his wife and three children when the war ended and stayed in Okehampton, working as a tailor. His three children, Francis William, Caroline Jane, and Theodore Felix, were all baptised on the same day, 31st. May 1818. The family are thought to have lived in Fore Street under the name of Hewet, and were evidently prosperous because they employed a servant.These details are recorded in the Census of January 1817; however, by 1828 they had moved elsewhere, and their names were no longer known in Okehampton. Charles Pie, a Surgeon and passenger aboard the French man o' war 'Esperance' when he was captured, was on parole first at Moretonhampstead, being transferred to Okehampton on 19th June 1810.

There were two prisoners by the name of De Lettre, one was Louis, a Lieutenant in the 27th. Infantry Regiment, captured at Vigo in Spain, who married Emma Jole. Joseph De Lettre was a merchant passenger on the French merchant vessel 'Le Furet', and Madame De Lettre was taken captive with him together with their little daughter, Eugenie, both of whom accompanied him to Okehampton. Eugenie was baptised there on 12th. December 1809. The following French baptisms are also recorded in the church registers:

21st. April 1811	Louis, son of Louis and Emma De Lettre (mentioned above).
22nd December 1811	Jean Baptis, son of Charles and Elizabeth Pie (mentioned above).
7th. August 1812	Claudius Phillip Peter, son of Claudius and Elizabeth Gujon.

Inevitably there were some illegitimate offspring, and it is known that in 1815, out of 21 children receiving Parish Relief, 4 had French fathers.

Dr. Young related how, many years ago, he was told by a Mr. Northam who lived in Painters Court (where the cinema now stands), that his great aunt had married an officer on parole, Baron Paravacini, and that he had been visited by their grandson who told him the Baron lived in a house in Fore Street belonging to a man called Lacey. Mr. Northam once did some work for Mr. Lacey and unearthed three old French coins in his garden. Several private soldiers who were probably servants to high ranking officers also lived in George Street he added.

In 1812 large numbers of officers on parole were moved from the south to the north of England and to Scotland. There were rumours of a plot for a general uprising of prisoners throughout the south and of plans to liberate the men on the hulks. Rumour or not, the Transport Board were

Okehampton parish churchyard. Stone path laid by French prisoners.

alarmed and took precautionary measures. Senior officers being transferred were separated from the other prisoners, nearly all of whom were sent to Oswestry. All the Okehampton prisoners were moved that year and the town lapsed into its former quiet state until 1815, when once again, as a result of Napoleon's escape from Elba and his bid to return to power during the 'Hundred Days', the town played host to the French. This time they came straight from the battlefields of Quatre Bras, Ligny, and the final decisive Battle of Waterloo. At least eleven of them are known to have fought in that last bloody battle, and they arrived in disarray with many wounded among them and not all of them soldiers – there were sailors too. From 5th. July 1815 to 16th. January 1816 a total of 66 officer prisoners were on parole in Okehampton.

The war finally ended a second time, never to be resumed, and the prisoners left for home. Apart from Vincent Gilles' signature in the castle and the graves of those who died in captivity, only the near forgotten stories and the names in the parish registers remain now to remind us of their stay. Somewhere in the churchyard are the graves of a French woman and three men:

Pierre Gast	Died 23rd. August 1810.
Abisene Coniare (possibly French).	Died 20th. November 1810.
Adelaide Barrin de Puyleaune	Died 18th. February 1811.
Armand Bernard	Died 26th. October 1815.

The exact location of their graves is not known. Two elderly Okehampton residents told the author the French headstones were pointed out to them as boys, and that they lie in the oldest part of the graveyard to the right of the lower path as you enter from the lower Lychgate. The author tried to find them but without success; it could be that they are so badly eroded the inscriptions are no longer legible (there are several of these), or maybe they have fallen and been removed. Luckily two inscriptions were recorded and are interesting. Two French nationals told the author a true interpretation of the words cannot be accurately made because some of the phrases are in 'Old French' and there are omissions which a French stonemason would not have made, rendering the texts incomplete. From the parish registers:

Armand Bernard. Died 26th. October 1815. (he was named as Frans Bernard on his headstone). The date indicates he died a free man, the French war having ended earlier that year; either he was awaiting repatriation or was too sick to be moved. The inscription on his headstone read:

> 'Cette Pierre Fut Elevee per Lamitie
> A La Memoire D'Armand Bernard
> Ne au Havre en Normandie a Calais a Madele Margot de
> Commerce. Decedee Prisonier de Guerre a Okehampton
> le 26 October 1815 Aged 33 Ans a Labris des Vertus
> ui Distinguainent la ve reposes en paix ombre tendre
> et Cherie'.

Translation: *'This stone was erected in Affectionate Memory of Armand Bernard, born in Havre in Normandy, married in Calais to Madele Margot. 2nd. Officer of Commerce. Died a Prisoner of War at Okehampton 26th. October 1815 aged 33 years. In the Shadow of the Virtue which distinguished your short life you Rest in Peace tender and beloved.* He was 2nd. Captain of the Merchant ship 'L'Emile'.

There is a French woman buried next to M. Bernard and there is a mystery concerning her presence at Okehampton. The inscription on her headstone named her as Adelaide Barrin de Puyleaune, but the register says she was Ann Duchaine, who died 18th.February 1811. We recall there was a family called Duchaine

Okehampton parish churchyard. Lower lychgate entrance and stone path laid by French prisoners on parole.

in the town from 1758 when Jacque Duchaine married Mary Rowe. Perhaps the family stayed in the area and it was a descendant who married the deceased Ann. Another possibility is that she was the wife of Bernard Duquene, Captain of the French Privateer 'L'Aventure', who was on parole in Okehampton from 15th. May 1809 to 2nd. January 1812, and that she either joined him from France or was taken prisoner with him. 'Duquene' was, and is, pronounced 'Duchaine', and it is well known that the clerks in those days often recorded what they heard without bothering to check on the spelling. The title on her headstone denotes she was a 'person of quality', and a child is mentioned. Here is the full inscription:

'Cr Cit Adelaide Barrin de Puyleaune de la Commune de Montravers des deux Sevres Nee le 31 Avril 1771. Decedee a Okehampton le 18 Fevre 1811 Fille le Legitme del Fare Notaire et Procravre de Machacoura ne de Nre.
Ici Repose la Mere et L'Enfant'.

Translation *'Adelaide de Puyleune of the Parish (or Town) of Montravers Dept. Des Deux Sevres (believed to be near Paris). Born 31st April 1771. Died at Okehampton 18th. February 1811. Legitimate Daughter of Del Farc, Notary of Machacoura, Born of Notre Dame. Here lie the Mother and Child'.*

In Ann Duchaine's case the wording suggests she might have been an aristocrat, perhaps in exile, but in any case a member of an important family. No mention is made of 'La Mere et L'Enfant' (Mother and Child) in the register, and we can only surmise she and her child died in childbirth and the infant would therefore not have been Baptised. It is a poignant and sad ending to what othewise may have been a romantic story.

NORTH TAWTON.

This little market town was once an important centre for the woollen industry and is situated off the popular tourist routes. It retains much of the character of its historic past and retains some evidence of the French officers who were sent here on parole. At the bottom of Fore Street stands a charming old house, set back from the road, which attracts the admiration of passers by on account of its quaint windows and small covered doorway.

Interestingly, the white front of the house is adorned with decorative plaster work attributed to the French prisoners of war who lived in the town on parole. The decoration takes the form of a climbing plant, very like a vine and adorned with leaves and flowers, curving in an attractive manner up the walls each side of the doorway. The present owner, like his predecessors, has gone to some trouble to maintain and preserve the Frenchmen's skill and artistry.

At the top of the High Street are some older houses where it is known some French officers were accommodated.

Decorated frontage to a house in North Tawton, by tradition the work of French prisoners on parole.

Close by, on the brow of the hill, there was once a group of houses known locally as 'The Barracks' where several French officers lived and which have since been demolished to make way for the little park that occupies the site now. The picturesque parish church is rendered more attractive by the pebbled patterns embedded in the paths approaching and surrounding the entrance. Local tradition has it this work was done by the French, demonstrating once more their practical ability, artistic talent, and the obvious good feeling that existed between them and the parishioners.

LAUNCESTON

The market town of Launceston was, until 1838, the County Town of Cornwall and because of its location, is familiar now to thousands of holidaymakers as the 'Gateway to Cornwall'. It boasts a Norman castle and the people who live there are, quite rightly, proud of its history. It was also a Parole town, on and off, since the Seven Years War with France (1756–1763) and from 1809 had a close relationship with Dartmoor Prison. For that reason it is included under a Dartmoor book title and some of the events that took place there are of exceptional interest.

Lawrence House Museum, where French officers on parole lived.

The story of the French officers on parole in Launceston centres around Castle Street which lies in the shadow of the castle and slopes steeply away from under it. It was once the most fashionable area of the town, housing its most prominent families, and it was with them that most of the Frenchmen were billeted. The fact that so many of them were accompanied by their personal servants is an indication of the high rank of those who were quartered here. Several elegant houses of that period survive in Castle street, one of which, Lawrence House, is now the home of Launceston Museum and has the distinction of providing accommodation for the Lord Mayor's Parlour. The rural views from the windows of this lovely house are stunning, and together with the richly decorated and ornate interior, must have contributed to a very pleasant way of life for the prisoners. We know that the townsfolk generally took a liking to them and this is reflected in the number of marriages that took place. They include the following from the parish registers:

1805.

| 18th. November | Michael Justin Herimon (Sojourner, Surgeon of the French Navy and prisoner of war in Launceston, to Mary Prout Lenn. |

22nd. December   Jean Pierre Geiger, Sojourner, to Ann Harris.

1808.

10th. July   Yves Pierre Marie Lemoine, French prisoner of war on Parole, to Jane Greed,

8th.   October   Yve Luncian, servant of a French officer on parole, to Ann Geffery.

22nd. October   John Baptiste Babron, French prisoner on parole, to Armenal Davey.

1809.

14th. January   John Gustave Alexander Perrinet, a French prisoner on parole, to Mary Kenner.

19th. February   Augustine Bellot, French prisoner on parole, to Deborah Harvey.

12th. September   Augustus Merie Riemel de Korene, French prisoner on parole, to Ann Doan.

16th. October   Pierre Noblet, servant of a French prisoner on parole, to Elizabeth Bray.

1812.

26th. January   Charles Phildebert Dupenchy, French prisoner on Parole, to Rebecca Spear.

Other hearts were captivated in other ways. *Robin's History of Launceston* (1883) tells us there was one French officer who stayed behind after the war and for many years was caretaker of the Wesleyan Chapel. In *The Memoires of Williain Pearce of Launceston* (1810) that gentleman relates how he sought converts among the Frenchmen (who, as we know, were Catholics – at least those who practised any form of religion at all) by giving them religious instruction and handing them religious tracts printed in French. His missionary zeal and personality got results, for there were several converts, one of whom came back to Launceston after being repatriated and "lived in the service of the chapel, eventually being buried in its graveyard." Could this man have been that same Wesleyan caretaker?

One of the Agents for the Launceston prisoners was a man called Spettigue, who by all accounts was an easy-going character, an attribute decidedly not in the best interests of his position. The number of escapes from the town and the laxity with which he acted became so well known several prisoners at Tavistock applied to be transferred there. In 1812 the authorities were obliged to move 37 prisoners to Hawick because of the numerous escape attempts. The wonder of it was he was allowed to retain his position for he had the distinction of being the only Agent detected charging a 'commission' on money forwarded through him for certain officers. That same year had tragic consequences for Pierre de Romfort (or De la Roche), who was convicted of forgery, a rare offence among parole prisoners. He was hanged at Bodmin on 13th. April 1812.

Launceston town and castle

Launceston's most interesting and romantic 'guest' was a charming young officer called Louis Vanhille, a ship's Purser who was captured at sea on board the privateer 'Le Pandour' and arrived in the town on parole on 12th. May 1806. He came from a wealthy family, spoke excellent English, and was well mannered, courteous, artistic, and entertaining. Inevitably he was invited to country houses throughout the area and went as far afield as Tavistock and Wadebridge. (Mr. Spettigue must have turned a 'blind eye' or neglected his duties if he was unaware that one of his charges was wandering over the countryside more or less at will). Vanhille was also a 'hit' with the ladies, but his idyll ended when he fell foul of a fellow officer who denounced him as a potential escapee (which was probably true) and he was sent to Dartmoor prison in 1811. Before long he became acquainted with a Tavistock girl called Mary Ellis, a market trader, one of several who attended the prison every day to barter or sell poultry, vegetables and the like. She supplied him with suitable clothing and in August 1812 he boldly made his escape by simply walking out of the prison disguised as one of the market people. Amazingly, and almost certainly with help from his Launceston friends, he evaded capture for several weeks before making his way to Bristol and sailing for Jamaica on board a merchant vessel called the 'Jane', intending to make his way from there to the United States, a neutral country, and thence home to France. He was unlucky. The authorities in Jamaica were suspicious of him and under questioning his identity was revealed and he was sent back to England. There was no parole for him this time and he spent the rest of the war a prisoner aboard one of the Chatham prison ships.

French officers' beer account book.
Courtesy of Lawrence House Museum

Launceston has managed to preserve some interesting relics of the Frenchmen's stay and these can be seen in the Lawrence House Museum. The house itself has some exquisite plaster work on the ceilings, some of which is said to have been executed by the French, and on display in the museum are a trio of figures carved from the vertebrae of an ox and cleverly painted, also attributed to them. The prisoners everywhere were renowned for their skill in modelling and a fine example of their art can be seen in the form of the hull of a ship with miniature cannons, constructed entirely from meat bones. For some reason the work remained unfinished (maybe the war came to an end first) but it is an admirable piece for all that. The officer's Beer Account Book survives but unfortunately all the pages are missing; they are thought to have been torn out and issued as receipts when payments were made. There are some paintings too. One of them depicts a charming view of Launceston, in black and white, by a French artist named J.B.Louvel, and there is an equally charming message underneath addressed to a Mr. James, to whom it was given – '...(may) it remember to you that you have a friend in this town!' he wrote.

Another picture is a copy of 'Vue de Launceston', the original of which was painted by a French officer named Limue and dated 1st. May 1808. It has a connection with a pleasant little story with which to conclude our brief appraisal of a little known part of Launceston's history. During the summer of 1808 a lad called Pethick got into difficulties whilst swimming in the Kensey Pool (a deep pool close to the present day Bowling Club car park) and was on the point of drowning when his cries were heard by two French officers out for a stroll. Happily he was rescued by them and the two men were befriended by the boy's parents who engaged them as tutors in the French language for their children. Henry, the boy they saved, became so attached to them he visited them in France almost every year after the war. He grew up to be Doctor Henry Pethick, a well known and respected medical man in Launceston and it was he who bought the original painting 'Vue de Launceston', but unfortunately its present whereabouts is not known. The excellent copy hanging in the town's museum has another local connection however because the artist, Otto B. Peter, an Associate of the Royal Institute of British Architects, was the son of Launceston's former Town Clerk Mr. Richard Peter. The picture nevertheless manages to impart the colour and flair of the French painter of long ago.

VUE DE LAUNCESTON.

'Vue de Lanceston' by French officer Limue, who was living on parole in Launceston. This copy by Otto B. Peter of Launceston was painted in 1913. The whereabouts of the original is not known. Courtesy of Lawrence House Museum

THE FREEMASONS.

In the centre of Roscoff, a French town familiar to many thousands of travellers using the Brittany Ferries, stands the Church of Our Lady of Kroaz-Batz. Just inside the entrance there is a memorial plaque to Father Joseph who was Baptised there in 1729 and guillotined 64 years later in 1793 for *'sa fidelite a la foi Catholique'* (for adhering to the Catholic faith). It is but one example of how organisations like the Church were persecuted by the French Revolutionaries for criticising certain aspects of the regime. The Freemasons, because of their restricted membership and private ceremonies, were also suppressed, being regarded as potential plotters against the State. Ever fearful of treachery, the Revolutionary leaders held the French people in an iron grip, spies and informers were taken at their word, and many citizens were executed upon suspicion and very little evidence. When the worst excesses of 'The Terror' subsided, Napoleon Bonaparte rose to lead the nation and he was wise enough to understand that in order to unite the nation the people must have certain rights and freedoms, especially those of religion and other fellowships.

By the time he was elected First Consul for life in 1799, he felt confident the restrictions on various organisations could be abolished and they were. The French claim (without documentary proof) that he belonged to a family with strong connections to the Brotherhood. His father Charles, his brothers Lucien, Joseph, Jerome, and Louis were allegedly Masons as well as his three brothers-in-law. Furthermore, he himself, it is claimed, was initiated during the period the French occupied Egypt. Whether or not these claims are valid Napoleon certainly realised the value of supporting them, especially as many of his top generals and naval officers were Masons too. In any case history has often shown that when things are done openly and freely, rulers can, if necessary, take appropriate steps to control them. Consequently, when suppression of religious and other bodies was lifted (always providing the citizens' loyalty was to their country and to him), Napoleon was able, through his agents, to keep his hand on the 'pulse' of the nation. He also won the adulation of those he governed and unswerving devotion from his soldiers and sailors (during the Peninsula campaign many years later, a wounded soldier tossed his amputated arm into the air shouting *"vive L'Empereur!"*).

There were numerous Masonic Lodges in the regiments of the French army and on naval warships, made possible by a special decree known as 'Discretionary Ambulation' which simply meant the Lodges would officially exist wherever the soldiers or sailors happened to be, and more Lodges were set up in captivity. The question must now be asked: 'How was it possible for prisoners of war to hold such meetings, record their activities, and retain the discretion so essential to them?' Help could only have come from among their captors – the British Brothers. Again, how was this possible? The explanation lies in the concept of Freemasonry advocated by and practised under United Grand Lodge of England (founded in 1717) whose teachings include the following:

1. A Freemason's first duty is to be a good citizen and respect the laws of the country he lives and works in.

2. Membership is open to all races and creeds who acknowledge a faith in a Supreme Being, by whatever name that Being may be called. Consequently there are today devout Christians, Jews, and Muslims among the many faiths represented in the ranks of Freemasonry worldwide

3. Politics and Religion are not permitted to be discussed in the Lodge. Given these guidelines we can appreciate no law was broken, moral or civil, when the French Brothers in captivity received a helping hand.

The foremost authority on the French prisoner's Lodges, the late W. Brother John T.Thorp of Leicester spent most of his adult life researching them both at home and in France. He died in 1932 and bequeathed his fine collection of certificates to the Leicester Lodge of Research at Freemason's Hall, Leicester, of which he was a founder member. He was assisted by Bro. F.J.W.Crowe, formerly of Ashburton and who later moved to Torquay. Together they succeeded in tracing more than fifty Lodges founded by French prisoners of war up to 1814. Among them were the following:

Dartmoor Prison	De La Reunion (Reunited)
Plymouth (Mill Prison)	Des Amis Reunion (Reunited Friends)
Plymouth hulks (Bienfaisant)	De la Reunion (Reunited)
(St. Isadore)	De la Consolation des Amis Reunion (Consolation of United Friends)
Launceston	Consolante Maconne (Consoling Mason)
Okehampton	Not known
North Tawton	De la Paix Desiree (Desired Peace)
Ashburton	Des Amis Reunion a L'Orient d'Ashburton (United Friends at the Orient of Ashburton)

We now know there were Lodges in five out of six prison of war depots, thirty two in the parole towns, and six on the hulks. (The spirit lived on during other, later conflicts, World War II for example, when there were active Lodges among the Allies interned in German and Japanese P.O.W. camps). When they were disbanded, either at the end of the war or when members were transferred elsewhere, the records of their meetings, etc. were preserved and ultimately deposited in the French Lodges to which the leading members belonged, where they were discovered years later by researchers like Mr. Thorp. The records reveal an astonishing amount of detail about members' origins and military background, as well as their movements. Ensign Rihl for example, before being transferred to Moretonhampstead, was a member of the North Tawton Lodge, his signature and Masonic status appearing on the back of a certificate described in the North Tawton section of this chapter. From Moreton he was moved to Oswestry where his involvement with the Masons is again evident from another certificate issued there which bears his signature as a witness. Some brief observations concerning the Lodges in the aforementioned parole towns are of interest. The full texts of the certificates to be described are of significance only to Freemasons and have been curtailed for the benefit of the average reader.

For that which follows the author acknowledges his debt to the late Mr. Ron Chudley of Exmouth who was kind enough to supply much useful information and gave permission to use material from his own excellent booklet, published privately, entitled Our Brothers the Enemy, *a perusal of Freemasonry as practiced by the French prisoners of war.*

Ashburton.

It was inevitable that the little Dartmoor town where French officers (and latterly Americans) lived over a period of nearly sixty years should have had a Lodge among the prisoners. A certificate issued by Lodge 'Des Amis Reunion' to Paul Carcenac still exists and is thought to date from between 1810 and 1812. The wording on it is as follows:

'The very worshipful Lodge of St. John, under the distinctive name of United Friends, at the Orient of Ashburton, England... Paul Carcenac, Assistant Commissary (Purser) has worked amongst us to the entire satisfaction of the Master Masons. We therefore pray all Brethren... to receive him... and obtain for him such assistance as he needs, offering to reciprocate in similar circumstances, and obtaining a promise from him that as soon as possible after his return to France... (he joins)... a regular

Lodge duly recognised by the Orient'. This is evidently an Initiation Certificate and his imminent repatriation is hinted at. This valuable parchment document has a small tin box containing a red seal attached to it by a blue ribbon, and the accompanying drawing illustrates the seal. The Lodge also had its own medal.

This drawing of the seal of the prisoners' lodge 'United Friends at the Orient of Ashburton, England' was made by David Fisher Esq.
Reproduced by kind permission of the late Mr Ron Chudley.

In April 1814 a petition was addressed to United Grand Lodge, London, by a group of American officers on parole at Ashburton. It reads:

"Brethren,

we the undersigned, being ancient York Masons, take the liberty of addressing you with this petition for our relief, being American prisoners of war on parole at this place. We are allowed 10s. 6d. per week for our support. In this place we cannot get lodgings for less than 3s. per week, and from that to 5s. per week. Meat is constantly from 9d. to 1s. per pound and other necessaries in proportion. Judge Brethren how we live, for none of us have any means of getting money. Our clothes are wearing out, and God knows how long we shall be kept here. Many of us have been captured 9 or 10 months... we have had this in contemplation for some time but have deferred making application until absolute want has made it necessary. We therefor pray that you will take into consideration and provide some means for our relief You will please address your letter to Edwin Buckannon. We humbly remain your penniless Brethren,

Edwin Buckannon	William Miller
G.W.Barbank	Archd. Taylor Jnr.
Pierson Baldwin	Ezra Ober
William Smith	Janies Lans

John Schers"

We do not know if this eloquent plea was granted but the letter illustrates how much can be learned from it. Ashburton at this time must have been crammed with parole prisoners. The French war had not yet ended and Americans captured during the War of 1812 were arriving to make matters worse, this being reflected in their difficulty in obtaining suitable lodgings and the inflated food prices.

Okehampton.

That there were Freemasons active among the prisoners there is evident from a certificate issued from that town in 1810. However there is no record of a Lodge. The explanation could lie with the old French rule (quoting Mr. Thorp) 'that seven Master Masons in a town where there is no Lodge... may hold a meeting and elect officers. They are, from that moment, a 'Lodge en Instance' (a Provisional Lodge) and can work as such...' This was probably the case with the Okehampton Masons who signed the reproduced document which is in the care of the Library of United Grand Lodge, London and is an Initiation Certificate of an unusual design. It reads:

'We, the undersigned Masons... declare and certify that we have communicated the degree of Apprentice mason to... Jean Baptiste Anselm Mousnier, native of St. Jean D'Angeley, Dept. of Charente Inferieur, aged 40 years, Lieut. of the vessel Ch. Dre. (it was in fact the Corvette 'L'Oreste'). That his conduct and his principles are well known to us .... we have therefore delivered to him the present certificate which he has signed in our presence... executed at Okehampton, England...'
It is dated 1810.

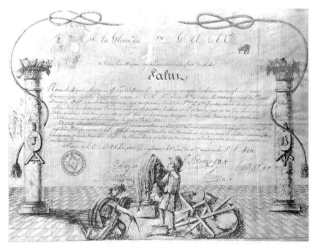

The Okehampton certificate issued to French Naval Lt. Jean Mousnier in 1810. The original measures 16 inches x 11½ inches on thick parchment.
Copy of original certificate kindly supplied by Freemasons Lodge of Research, Freemasons Hall, Leicester.

Moretonhampstead.

There is no evidence so far to suggest there was a prisoner's Lodge here, but as we already know, there were certainly Masons among those detained there – Ensign Rihl for one, and Lt. Quantin who was buried with Masonic Honours. In all probability there was a Lodge and the records have yet to be found. There was an English Lodge at Moretonhampstead, but it was 'warranted' and transferred to Sidmouth before the Frenchmen came and we do not know why.

North Tawton.

Mr. Thorp discovered a very handsome certificate emanating from Lodge 'De la Paix Desiree' which was well supported by the officers on parole in this peaceful little town. He described it as being of a most unusual design, and the illustration certainly bears that out. At the head is the Eagle of St. John and the symbol of Peace is represented by the Lion and the Lamb lying together at the foot. It was executed entirely by hand. The wording includes:

'We, the Masters and Officers of the W. Lodge of St. John, under the name of La Paix Desiree, regularly constituted and meeting at North Tawton, Devonshire… attest that Brother Antoine Darnal, native of Souillac, Dept. of Lot, is a member of our Lodge… and that his conduct, his manners and assiduity in his work..have made him worthy of recommendation… in token of which we have given his present certificate.

Done and delivered at our Lodge at North Tawton… 10th. March 1810'.

One of the signatures of endorsement is that of Ensign Jean Rihl who also endorsed another certificate at Oswestry four years later. A French Mason who was formerly at Okehampton, and who had Signed Lt. Mousnier's certificate there, added his signature to that of Darnal's whilst at Oswestry, and we may conclude all three were sent there in 1812 when large transfers of officers took place as mentioned earlier in this book.

Launceston.

As this was one of the oldest parole towns it was more than likely a Masonic Lodge would appear there and such is the case. Two certificates issued on behalf of 'La Consolante Maconne' are in existence. The first of these was given to Jean Joint and is written, like so many others elsewhere, entirely in French. On the back are endorsements from various Lodges he visited on his return home after the war. Curiously, there are the names of three Englishmen, or more probably Cornishmen, also inscribed on the back.

Certificate issued by Lodge 'La Paix Desiree' at North Tawton to Frenchman Antoine Darnal and dated 10 May 1810.

Courtesy of Freemasons Hall, Leicester

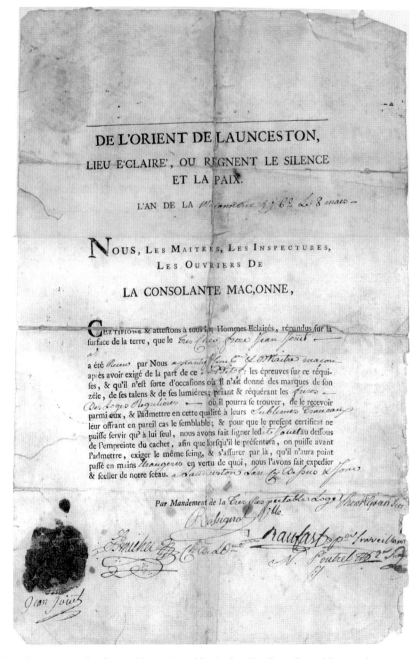

DE L'ORIENT DE LAUNCESTON,

LIEU E'CLAIRE', OU REGNENT LE SILENCE ET LA PAIX.

L'AN DE LA *Maçonnerie ... 6. Le 8 mars —*

NOUS, LES MAITRES, LES INSPECTURES, LES OUVRIERS DE

LA CONSOLANTE MAÇONNE,

CERTIFIONS & attestons à tous les Hommes Eclairés, répandus sur la surface de la terre, que le *Très cher frère Jean Jouet* a été *Reçu* par Nous *apprentif compon & Maître maçon* après avoir exigé de la part de ce *Très cher frère* : les épreuves sur ce requifes, & qu'il n'est sorte d'occasions où il n'ait donné des marques de son zéle, de ses talens & de ses lumiéres; priant & requérant les *frères* *des Loges Regulieres* — où il pourra se trouver, de le recevoir parmi eux, & l'admettre en cette qualité à leurs *Sublimes Travaux* leur offrant en pareil cas le semblable; & pour que le present certificat ne puisse servir qu'à lui seul, nous avons fait signer led*it Jouet* au dessous de l'empreinte du cachet, afin que lorsqu'il le présentera, on puisse avant l'admettre, exiger le même seing, & s'assurer par là, qu'il n'aura point passé en mains *étrangeres* en vertu de quoi, nous l'avons fait expedier & sceller de notre sceau. *à Launceston l'an & jour que dessus*

Par Mandement de la *Très Respectable Loge Vhonllipan les*

Rasigned 1766.

Jean Jouet

They were:

Samuel Harris of Smallacombe, Devon, Francis Rodd of Trebartha Hall, Cornwall and John Molesworth of Pencarrow, Cornwall

All of them were respectable persons who were known to the local Gentry. We can only surmise the mention of their names by M. Joint would have been of some help in procuring assistance should the need have arisen. (The first English Lodge, later disbanded, was not established in Launceston until three years afterwards, so there is no connection there). More than likely they were friends he had made whom he wished to remember – they would not have been the only persons of respectability to befriend officer prisoners. It reflected badly on the town later when it became notorious for the number of attempted and often successful escapes, many of which could only have been undertaken with help from its citizens. As a result, when application was made to United Grand Lodge in 1809 for an English Lodge to be re-established there, it was refused for that very reason, an indication of the great care the organisation took to prevent its good name being tarnished.

The second of the two Launceston certificates was issued to an Englishman (or was he Cornish?) Mr. Robert Martin. According to Mr. Thorp this was a very unusual occurrence, only two other instances of this kind being known about. Furthermore, and even more unusual, La Consolante Lodge was the only one known to have produced certificates with the texts written in French or English, depending on the nationality of the recipient. Most Lodges were prepared to transcribe the wording into both languages if necessary, but the unique fact is that at Launceston the Lodge actually had two printing plates made up, one in French the other in English. Mr. Martin was not alone in being honoured in this way because both his certificate and that of M. Joint (both men were already Masons when they received them by the way) bear the signatures of two more English or Cornish men, Mr. Thomas Green and Mr. W.Rowe who were certainly members of the Lodge, and there were probably others. Mr. Martin was the organist at the Parish Church of St. Mary Magdalene and was buried in the churchyard when he died.

It is hoped these notes on the French prisoner's Lodges have been as interesting to the reader as they have to the author, who gleaned the information from many sources, mostly from members of the Brotherhood whose courtesy and help was unfailing. Without the records and memorabilia stored in their archives a vast amount of knowledge concerning those turbulent times would be lost or at best forgotten.

From the **Eaſt** of LAUNCESTON,

An enlighten'd Place, where reign Silence and Peace,

1ᵗ April .... In the Year of MASONRY 5762.

E, the MASTERS, INSPECTORS, and LABOURERS, of this Regular Lodge, entitled *Conſolante Maçonne*, certify and atteſt to all Enlightened Men throughout the World, that the Brother *Robert Martin of Launceston in the County of Cornwall Organist, a Master Mason Perfect, Irish Scot and English Master*

was by us received and admitted to the Degree of *apprentice fellow craft Master Scotch Mason* after having given the neceſſary Proofs; and who, on every Occaſion, has ſhewn his Underſtanding and Zeal: We therefore pray and require the Brethren of every Regular Lodge to which he may happen to come, to receive him among them, and to admit him to their ſublime Labours, we promiſing to pay the ſame Reſpect to them.   And that this Certificate may ſerve no other Perſon, we've obliged the ſaid Brother to ſign beneath the Seal, that when this may be preſented to any Lodge, before they admit him, they may demand the ſame Sign, to ſatisfy themſelves that the Certificate belongs to the Perſon who preſents it.   In Virtue of which we have ſigned this, and cauſed it to be ſealed with the Seal of our Lodge.

Robt. Martin

By Order of this Worſhipful Lodge,

Another certificate from the Launceston Lodge, and an unusual one, being issued to a Launceston man, Mr Robert Martin. He was not only a Mason but organist of the Parish church of St Mary Magdalene and was buried in the churchyard.

SUMMARY

Westcountry auction rooms sometimes have superb models and hand made knick knacks for sale – a legacy of the French and American prisoners who lived, and sometimes died, among us, although they are nearly always attributed (unfairly perhaps) to the French alone. Other articles, often the best there are, remain in private hands and are rarely seen. Museums all over the country have examples of their handiwork and one of the most spectacular of these is in Plymouth City Museum, an excellent model of a full rigged man o'war, a popular subject among the prisoners and a favourite

Bone model of British 'Third Rate' ship of the line, attributed to French prisoners of war. PHOTO: Reproduced by permission of Plymouth City Museum and Art Gallery.

An intricate model of a guillotine together with enactment of an execution, made entirely from bone by French prisoners of war. PHOTO: Reproduced by permission of Plymouth City Museum and Art Gallery.

for buyers in those times. It is hard to believe this lovely object, made to scale and with every detail of line and rigging reproduced to perfection, was made from meat bones and human hair. The work was done with home made tools, a lot of improvisation, and infinite patience – but then, the manufacturers had all the time in the world. Other beautifully made models include churches, toys, snuffboxes and trinkets. The ship model at Plymouth described above is accompanied by a representation of the infamous French guillotine, exquisitely made of bone, replete with miniature figures enacting the dramatic scene on the scaffold.

Pin cushion made by French officer at Dartmoor Prison from uniform tunic and silk epaulettes.

The pin cushion illustrated here was made by a French officer from material taken from his uniform tunic and embroidered with silken strands taken from his shoulder epaulettes. This particular officer was befriended by Mr. Richard Edwards, a Prince Town baker, who delivered bread every day to Dartmoor Prison, and he was the recipient of a total of four similar cushions, one each for his four daughters. Two of these beautiful creations are in existence today and the one shown here is by kind permission of one of his descendants who keeps it lovingly wrapped and like new – a real family treasure and definitely not for sale.

Another example of the Frenchmen's work was sold some years ago at Mr. Robin Fenner's auction rooms in Tavistock. It was a snuff box carved entirely from bone and embossed on the lid was a bust of the Emperor Napoleon, perfectly executed and instantly recognisable. One of the most stunning objects of this kind to pass through Mr. Fenner's hands was a 'Spinning Jenny', measuring a mere four by one and a half inches, made entirely of minute pieces of bone, and in full working order. The tiny hand wheel underneath operated miniature cogs which in turn activated the spinning wheel and the loom, whilst at the same time a female figure, also made from bone, moved her head and arms in unison as if at work with the machine. This magnificent piece attracted wide interest and the admiration of all who saw it. The successful bidder was a representative for a French museum, surely the most appropriate destination for it.

Other artefacts constructed from odd bits of metal or bone and ranging from items such as those described above to unfinished pieces of carved bone, shirt buttons made of the same, and occasionally uniform buttons, are uncovered from time to time on prison land on Dartmoor and in the gardens of houses in Princetown and other towns close by the moor. A relic from Moretonhampstead turned up at Messrs. Rendell's auction rooms in Ashburton as recently as 1994. The reader will recognise the connection as related in the following newspaper report from *The Evening Herald* (Plymouth) 26th January 1994:

AN HISTORIC TIMEPIECE

An unusual pocket watch with a fascinating past involving Dartmoor and a French prisoner from the Napoleonic Wars, will be auctioned tomorrow at Rendell's in Ashburton.

The fine, 18th century cased watch taken into the saleroom by a local owner, set the auctioneers off on a Lovejoy type adventure across Dartmoor.

They learned, after locating a plaque on a church wall, researching the history of Dartmoor Prison, and talking to historians and clergymen, that the timepiece originally belonged to a French officer imprisoned at Princetown – Louis Ambroise Quantin, a Lieutenant with the Regiment du Corps Imperial d'Artillerie de Marine.

After being released on parole at Moretonhampstead, he died aged 33, in April 1810. References to him are contained in the parish church there, including a plaque commemorating his death.

The watch, which has several unusual features, including an exposed jewelled balance wheel on the dial, is likely to sell for £800–£1,200.

Reproduced by kind permission of the Editor, *Evening Herald*, Plymouth.

Napoleon's soldiers and sailors were recruited in the countries he conquered as well as in France, often by ballot, thus in the armed forces there were representatives of all trades and occupations, men of culture and learning, artists and writers, as well as professional soldiers and sailors who enlisted on a wave of enthusiasm generated by the charisma of the Emperor himself. It was truly a 'people's army' and this helps to explain how such a wealth of talent was evident among the prisoners. The British, by comparison, also recruited to the lower ranks by ballot, but those who were balloted could pay for a substitute to go in their stead, usually a pauper or a hard-up labourer. Royal Navy shortages were made good by criminal 'volunteers' from the gaols and by impressment. Britain's ordinary soldiers and sailors were therefore drawn almost exclusively from the lowest classes whilst the skilled workers stayed at home. The American captives were no less skilled than their French counterparts although examples of their work are rarer because their war with us lasted less than two years, compared to the French war of eleven years duration from the ending of the Treaty of Amiens to Napoleon's exile to Elba.

When we consider the thousands of prisoners who were on parole in towns throughout Britain, and who left their mark not just in tangible things, but in affairs of the heart, it scarcely seems possible that today so little appears to be known about their stay. Yet there is a growing awareness that something unique and exciting took place, much of it fostered by television series and films depicting dashing young men in colourful uniforms performing daring and often chivalrous acts. These, together with a number of romantic novels about those times, contain thoroughly researched material and project an image of those times very close to the truth. If this glimpse of the past arouses public interest, then this book will have served its purpose – and who knows how much is still to be discovered?

Working model of a Spinning Jenny made out of meat bones by French prisoners of war – sold to a French museum.
Courtesy of Mr Robin Fenner

BIBLIOGRAPHY

The Story of Dartmoor Prison by Basil Thomson (W.Heinemann 1907).

Memorials of Old Devonshire by F.J. Snell.

Ashburton the Dartmoor Town (Pamphlet) by Francis Pilkington 1978.

French Prisoners of War by Cecil Torr (Westcountry Studies M.S. 40).

Prisoners of War in Britain by Francis Abell (Oxford University Press 1914).

History of Plymouth and its Neighbourhood by C.W.Brachen, B.A., F.E.S. 1931.

The War of 1812 by Donald Hickey (University of Illinois Press).

Lawrence House, Launceston by H. Spencer Toy (Launceston Borough Council 1971).

Born in Blood (Lost secrets of Freemasonry) by John L.Robinson (Guild Publishing 1990).

Our Brothers the Enemy by R.Chudley (Published privately).

French Prisoners Lodges by W.Bro. John T.Thorp (1900).

Napoleon – Master of Europe by Alistair Horne (Weiderfield & Nicolson).

The Emperor's Last Island by Julia Blackburn (Mandarin Books).

The Fatal Cruise of the Argus by Ira Dye (Airlife Publishing Ltd., Shrewsbury).

Notes & Queries (Various).